A Forest Friends Book

Puppy's Visit

a story about fairness

A Friendship Series
By Leslie Falconer
Pictures by Chris Lensch

First published by Experience Early Learning Company
7243 Scotchwood Lane, Grawn, Michigan 49637 USA

Text Copyright © 2019 by Experience Early Learning Co.
Printed and Bound in the USA

ISBN: 978-1-937954-60-4
Visit us at www.ExperienceEarlyLearning.com

Puppy was visiting the Forest Friends!
Everyone loved to play with Puppy
so they took turns.

Mouse played
with Puppy.

Bear played
with Puppy.

Bird played
with Puppy.

Owl played
with Puppy.

Bee played
with Puppy.

Otter played
with Puppy.

Fox played
with Puppy.

Bunny played
with Puppy.

Finally it was
Raccoon's turn!

4

But it was late and Puppy had to go home. Raccoon did not get a turn.

Raccoon was sad, and the other
Forest Friends felt badly, too.

"I'm sorry. It wasn't fair that you didn't get a turn," Fox said to Raccoon. This made Raccoon feel better.

The next week, Puppy came back to visit. Everyone was excited, but Raccoon was worried that he wouldn't get to play with Puppy again.

Fox saw Raccoon and had a good idea. "Today instead of taking turns, let's all play together with Puppy."

Everyone cheered. Fox gave Raccoon a stick to toss to Puppy. Puppy ran around and then jumped into Raccoon's arms.

The End